New stars bright

Angels delight

Being, truth, and beauty

Light and life.

Imperfect though,

Far from high,

Give Glory to the Lord.

Lawrence Nusbaum, Artist

Saatchiart.com
Fineartamerica.com — art

Createspace.com
Amazon.com — books

Santa Fe, New Mexico

lawnus@peoplepc.com

Facebook 505 820 0174

Lawrence Nusbaum copyright 2017

Lawrence 1138xb

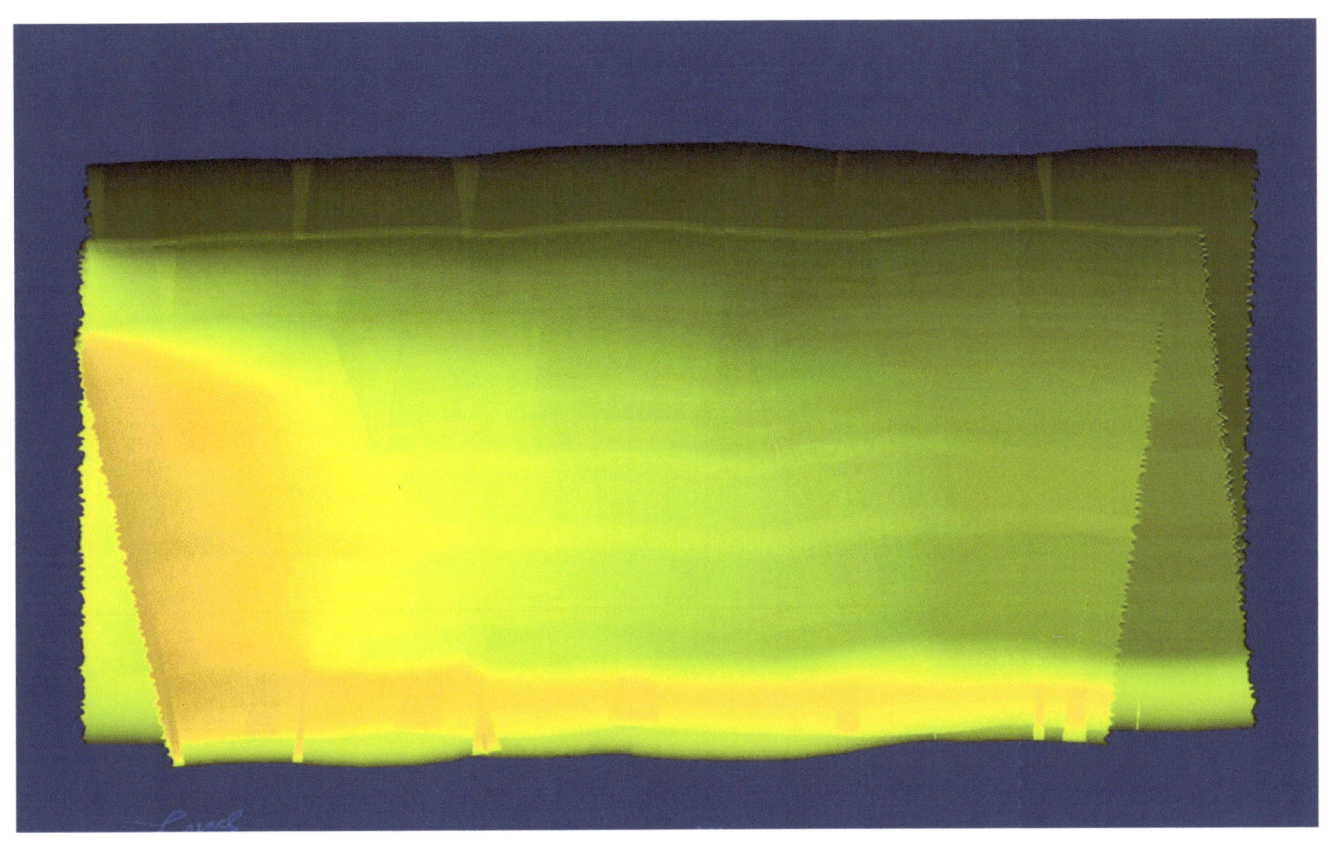

Lawrence 718xc

Lawrence 1081x

Lawrence 62xb

Lawrence 1026xb

Lawrence 298x

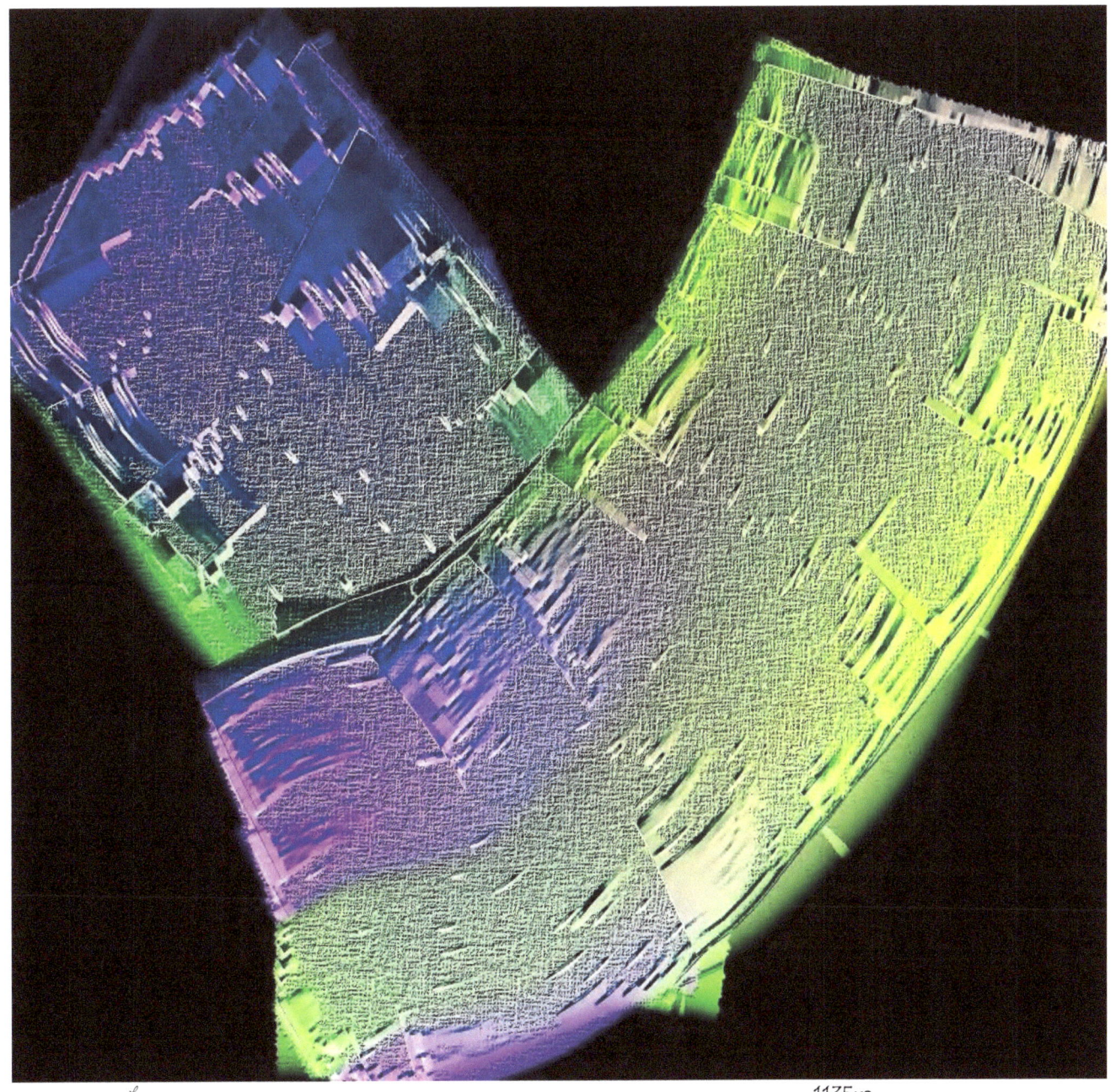

Lawrence 1135xa

Lawrence 1054xa

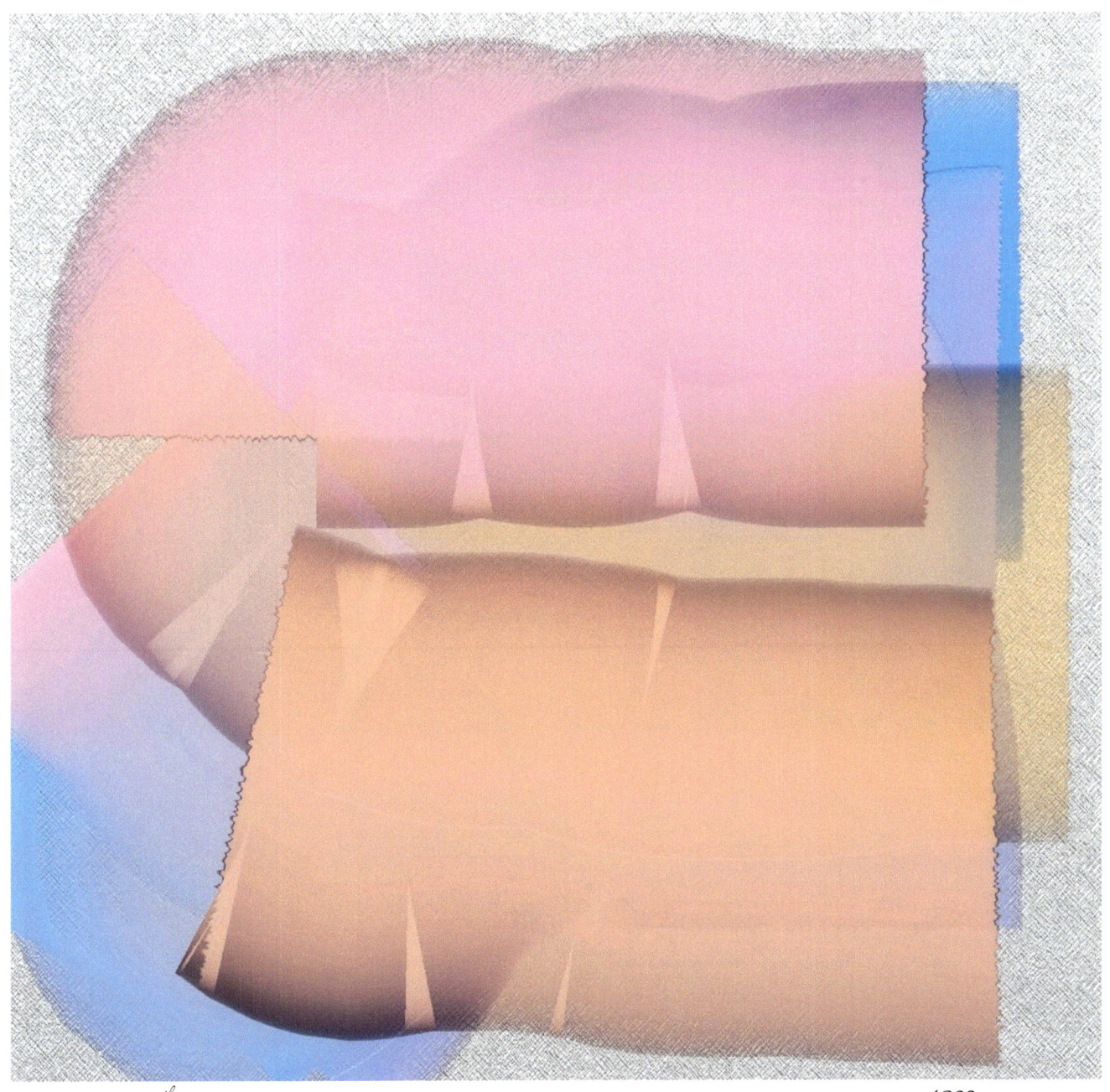

Lawrence 1099x

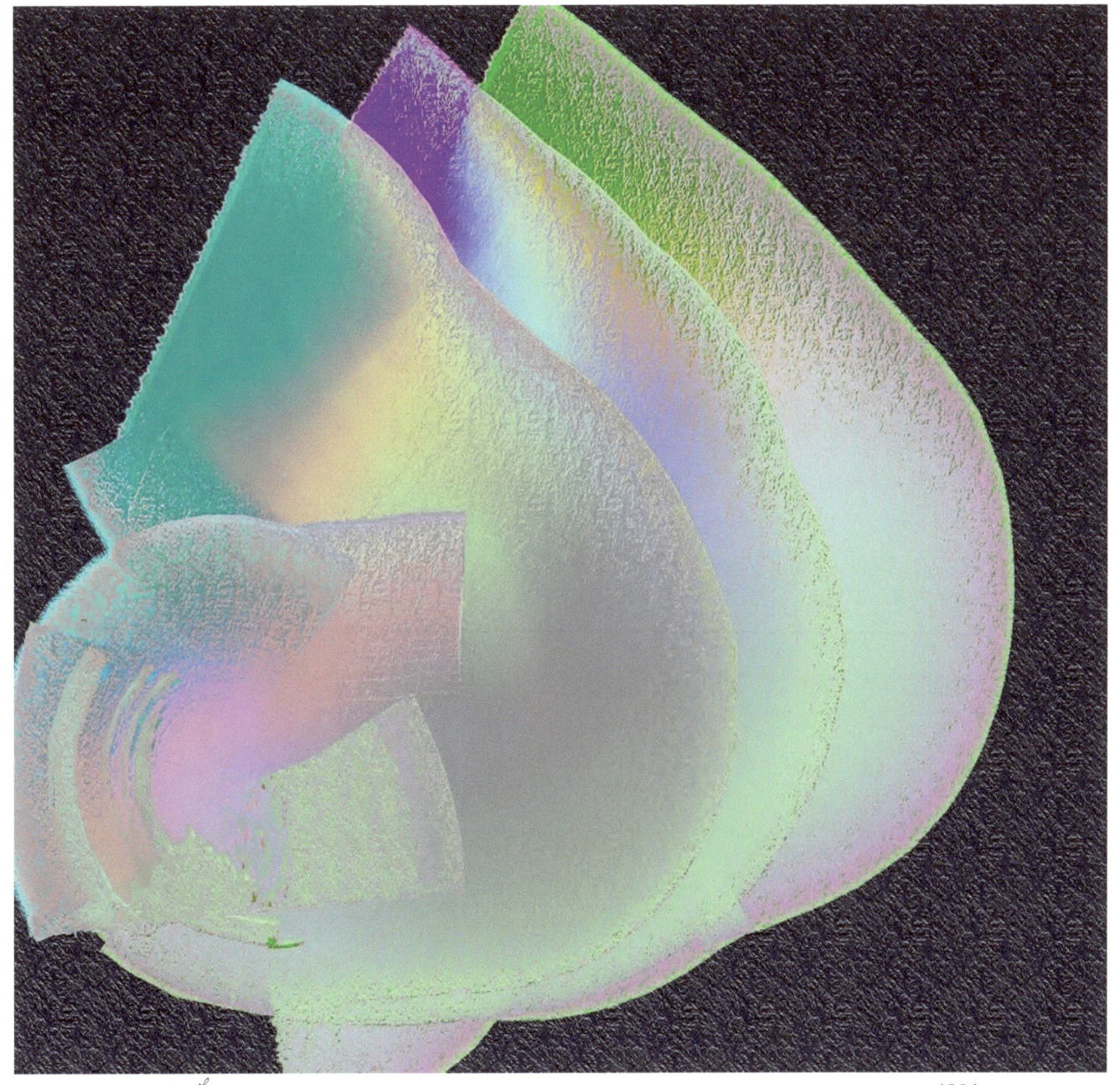

Lawrence 1084xc

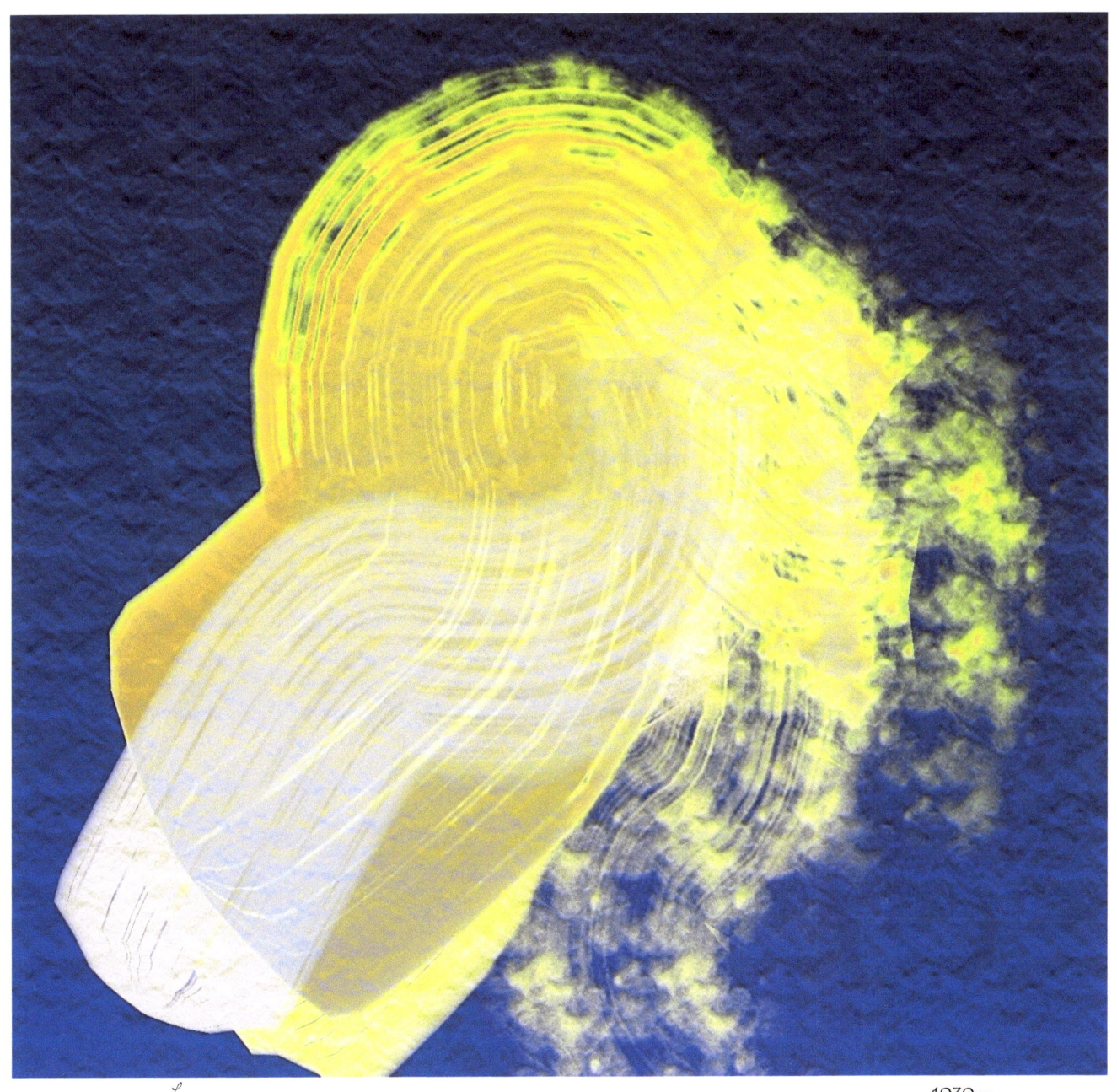

Lawrence 1030xe

Lawrence 585xc

Lawrence 810xa

Lawrence 145xc

Lawrence 355xd

Lawrence 386xba

Lawrence 177x

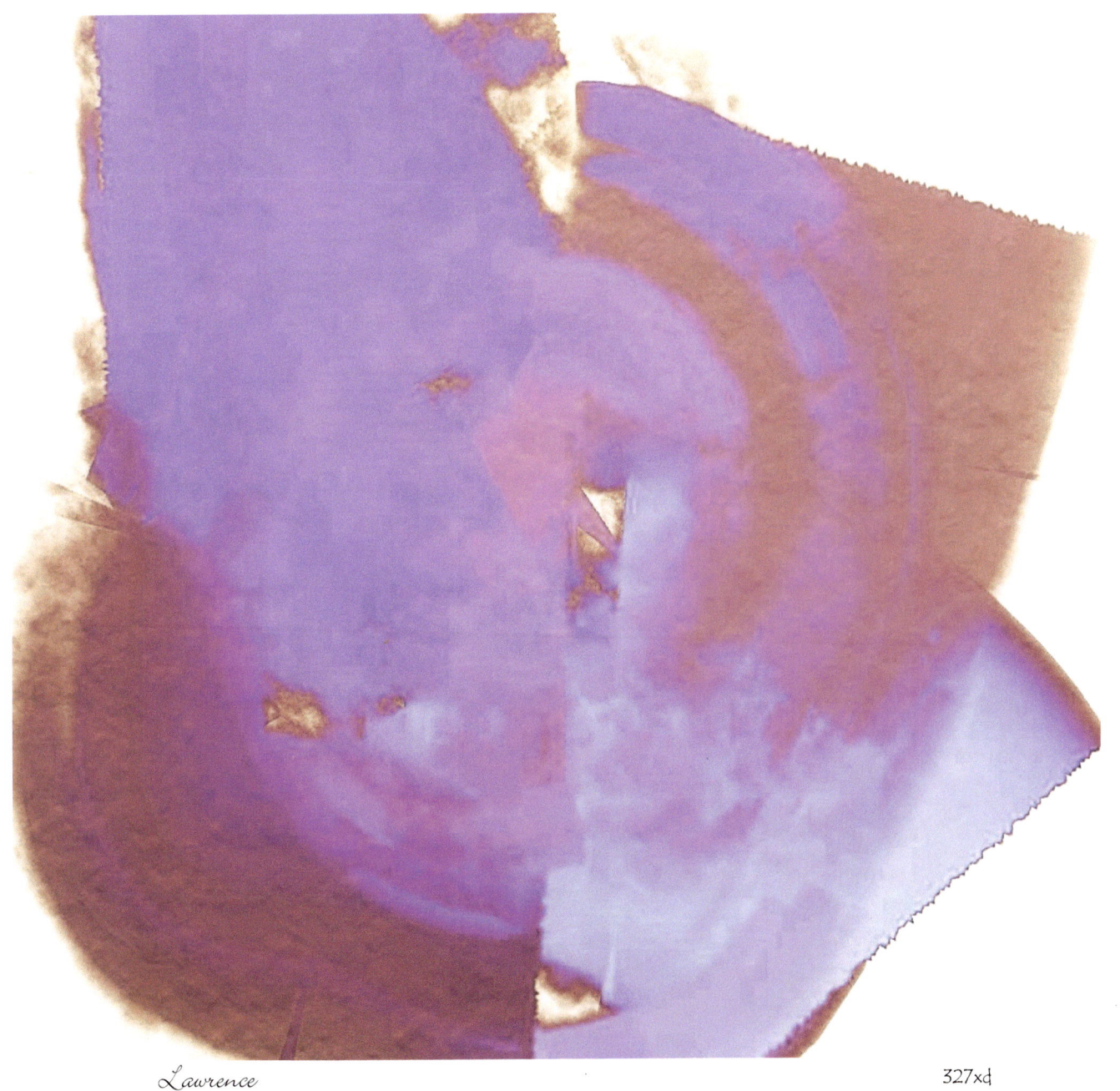

Lawrence 327xd

Lawrence 536xd

Lawrence 546xad

Lawrence 579xb

Lawrence 804xb

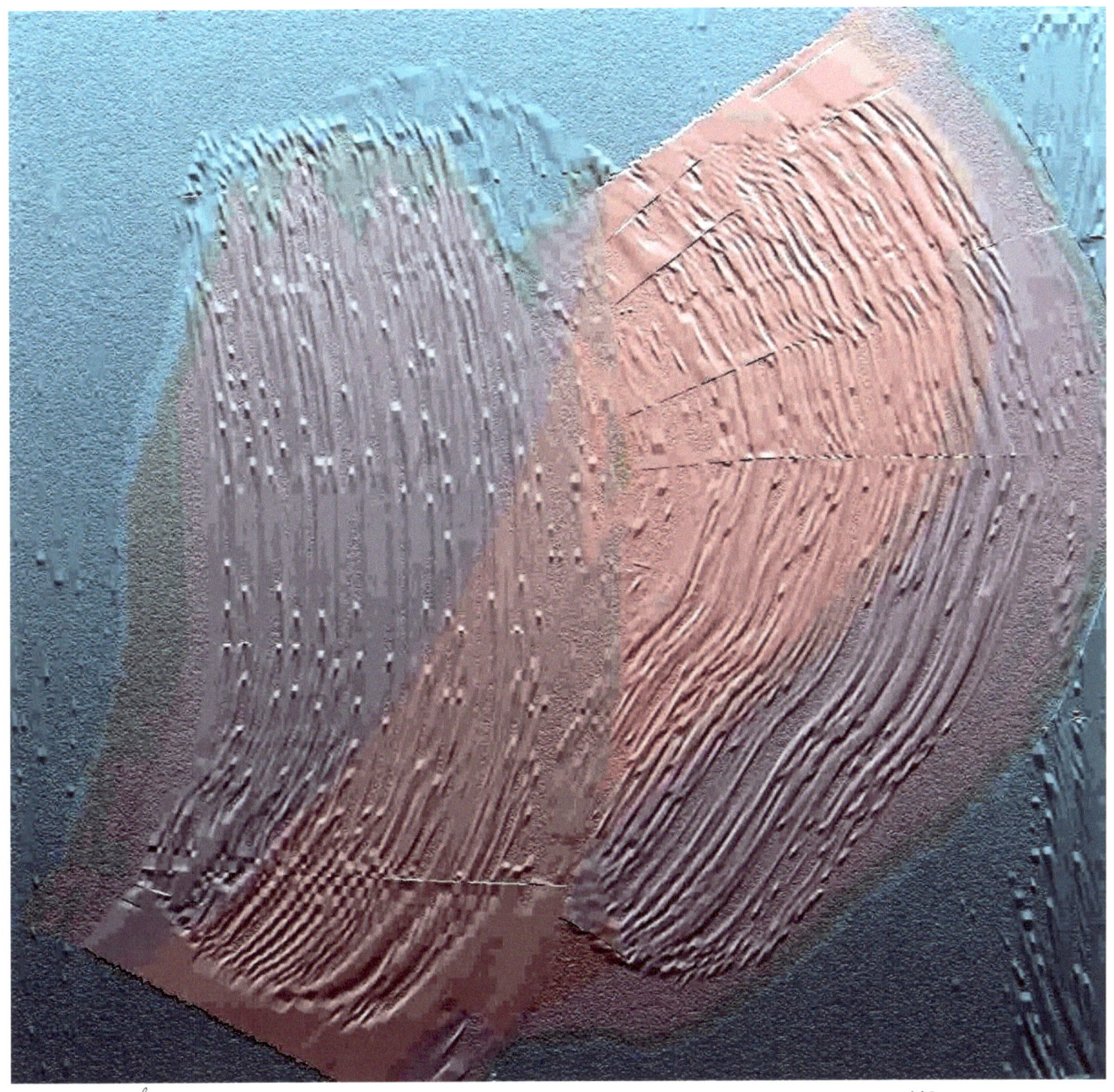

Lawrence 668x

Lawrence 530x

By the year 1983 Lawrence had received a degree in Counseling Psychology and Studio Art from the University of Missouri adding to his previous studies in English, History, Psychology, Philosophy and Theology at Immaculate Conception Seminary, Conception, Missouri (1960-1968). An appreciation for nature, begun and nurtured on his father's farm in Kansas, is now nourished on the pinon filled hills and mountains; on the blue, blue skies, hot sun, cool winds; on the dry, richly marbled, rocky earth; on the varied traditions of Santa Fe New Mexico.